BROADWAY FAVORITES

Solos and String Orchestra Arrangements
Correlated with Essential Elements String Method

Arranged by
LLOYD CONLEY

Welcome to Essential Elements Broadway Favorites! This book is designed to be used as a complement to the STRING ORCHESTRA arrangements. These easy percussion parts may be played by members of the string orchestra or by adding one or two percussion students.

ISBN 0-634-01858-2

HAL•LEONARD®
CORPORATION
7777 W. BLUEMOUND RD. P.O. BOX 13819 MILWAUKEE, WI 53213

Visit Hal Leonard Online at
www.halleonard.com

00868045

From THE SOUND OF MUSIC
EDELWEISS

PERCUSSION
Bells

Lyrics by OSCAR HAMMERSTEIN II
Music by RICHARD RODGERS
Arranged by LLOYD CONLEY

BEAUTY AND THE BEAST

PERCUSSION
Triangle, Sus. Cym.

Lyrics by HOWARD ASHMAN
Music by ALAN MENKEN
Arranged by LLOYD CONLEY

rit. opt.

00868045

Disney Presents THE LION KING: THE BROADWAY MUSICAL

CIRCLE OF LIFE

PERCUSSION
Afuche (Maracas), 3 Pitched Tom-Toms

Music by ELTON JOHN
Lyrics by TIM RICE
Arranged by LLOYD CONLEY

00868045

I DREAMED A DREAM

PERCUSSION
Ride Cym., Snare Drum, Bass Drum

Music by CLAUDE-MICHEL SCHÖNBERG
Lyrics by ALAIN BOUBLIL,
JEAN-MARC NATEL and HERBERT KRETZMER
Arranged by LLOYD CONLEY

00868045

From THE PHANTOM OF THE OPERA

THE PHANTOM OF THE OPERA

PERCUSSION
Ride Cym., Snare Drum, Bass Drum, Sus. Cym.

Music by ANDREW LLOYD WEBBER
Lyrics by CHARLES HART
Additional Lyrics by RICHARD STILGOE and MIKE BATT
Arranged by LLOYD CONLEY

From MISS SAIGON

SUN AND MOON

PERCUSSION
Oriental Drum (Tom-Tom), Triangle

Music by CLAUDE-MICHEL SCHÖNBERG
Lyrics by ALAIN BOUBLIL and RICHARD MALTBY JR.
Additional Lyrics by MICHAEL MAHLER
Adapted from original French Lyrics by ALAIN BOUBLIL
Arranged by LLOYD CONLEY

00868045

From the Musical CABARET
CABARET

PERCUSSION
Ride Cym., Snare Drum, Bass Drum

Words by FRED EBB
Music by JOHN KANDER
Arranged by LLOYD CONLEY

GET ME TO THE CHURCH ON TIME

Words by ALAN JAY LERNER
Music by FREDERICK LOEWE
Arranged by LLOYD CONLEY

PERCUSSION
Chimes (Opt. Bells)

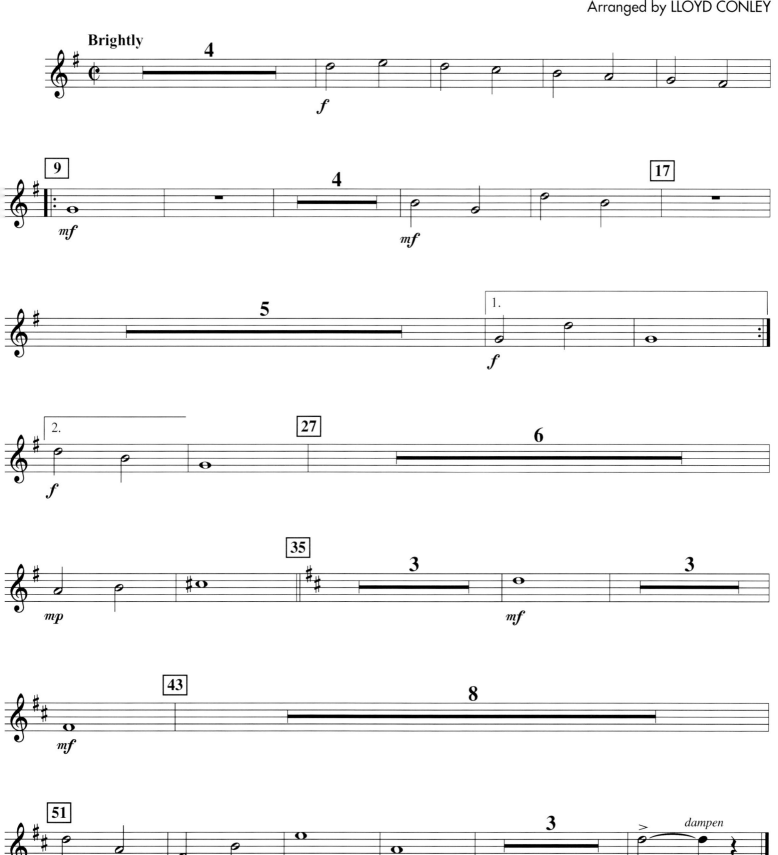

From JOSEPH AND THE AMAZING TECHNICOLOR DREAMCOAT

GO GO GO JOSEPH

PERCUSSION
Ride Cym., Hi-Hat, Snare Drum, Bass Drum

Music by ANDREW LLOYD WEBBER
Lyrics by TIM RICE
Arranged by LLOYD CONLEY

MEMORY

Music by ANDREW LLOYD WEBBER
Text by TREVOR NUNN after T.S. ELIOT
Arranged by LLOYD CONLEY

PERCUSSION
Bells, Sus. Cym.

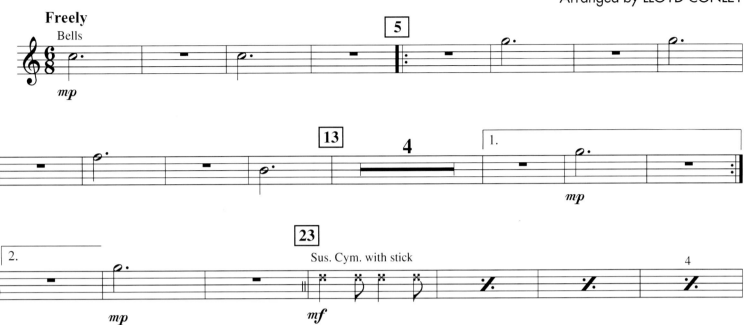

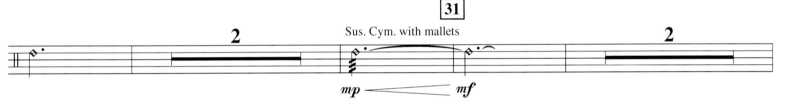

From Meredith Willson's THE MUSIC MAN

SEVENTY SIX TROMBONES

PERCUSSION
Snare Drum, Bass Drum, Sus. Cym.

By MEREDITH WILLSON
Arranged by LLOYD CONLEY